About the Author

Victoria was born in Cambridge in 1979 and brought up and educated in the Cotswolds, later moving to Cheshire before returning back home in 2016.

Always interested in spiritual studies and human behaviour, Victoria wanted to go to astrology school. Settling on a more mainstream route of psychology, media studies and a computer course, it was that which led to her first full time job in estate agency. For years working in different towns north and south, and later in private medical insurance, accompanying these moves combined a passion for travelling. Victoria started her own business in 2014 in Crystal Healing and Reiki and is now seeking a spiritual home in Spain.

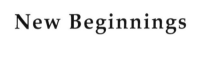

New Beginnings

Victoria Day-Joel

New Beginnings

Olympia Publishers
London

www.olympiapublishers.com
OLYMPIA PAPERBACK EDITION

A CIP catalogue record for this title is
available from the British Library.

ISBN: 978-1-78830-789-5

First Published in 2020

Olympia Publishers
Tallis House
2 Tallis Street
London
EC4Y 0AB

Printed in Great Britain

Dedication

Miss Blue Skies with Watery Eyes
dedicates 'New Beginnings' to
Mr Big Hair Heavy Rain.

Dear Sammy,
You've felt the words
you've yet to read
through me

My heart bursts with light
Thinking of the love I feel for you.

Love Victoria.

Acknowledgements

Becky Brough photography

Karen Daye & Eileen Franklin for their contribution to
Mother Moon

The sights we encounter as we walk or drive by on a daily basis however beautiful,
become something we pass without thought.
A mind occupied by chaos is just getting from A to B,
where every day scenery blends into the background.
A mind occupied by stillness will see the beauty in the colour of the leaves, shapes in the tree, embrace the scenery and notice subtlety.
Being in the moment is a blink of an eye, presence and awareness will see those magic moments.

New Season

First days of spring have sprung.
Lingering firewood scents the dewy air,
Rain washes a pastel hue;
Lining and lightening the stonework.
The sun will keep rising,
Promising to shine through.

I've noticed a change or perhaps a change is coming?
It's not all you can see, the change is happening
internally.
Dissatisfaction with the day to day, excitement for the
future getting carried away.
For now, I'll let the smell of smoky firewood clear
unwanted thoughts away.

<u>Cheltenham</u>

I park near the roundabout filled with flowers.
When school's out the circus is green space with trees.
Seagulls are the morning sirens;
Imagining Sea in this spa town with regency.

Horses bring a cosmopolitan community;
Gold cup wishes, four leaf clovers.
Betting slips line streets
like glitter replacing leaves,
On the usual concrete scenery.

The opposite way walks a man in green,
And a red cap pensioner by the Holst museum.
Always believe you walk the path of gold.
This is the town where I found jewels to my crown.

<u>Saturday</u>

As the morning sun beats,
I walk the parks and streets.
The breeze creates surround-sound bird symphonies.
I'm on the run from mundanity;
Walking in the grass with no shoes on.
Sleeping with the same clothes on.
Who made the rules?
I'll buy an ice-cream and become a tourist in my
hometown.

*Without an open mind or making changes, you cannot
grow or embrace your truest path; change is
inevitable. Through intent my thoughts had become
fixed.*
*I thought I had no time to be in a relationship, set on a
single life with a focus, a full-time job, a therapies
business and getting ready for the marketing of my
first book.*

*Yet sometimes I would wonder, will I find someone
who can tame my restless nature? Why do I want to be
tamed? It will take another untamed to understand
me!*

Two Years Ago

We used to see each other
walking in the morning,
Strangers exchanging pleasantries.
You held the metro coming back from the station,
I passed in office wear, 'nice hair, nice shoes';
Making my day more colourful.

I was meeting a friend for lunch at an American retro-
style diner close to work.
That morning a little voice in my head was guiding me
to take a business card;
without any further thought I did and shot out the
door.

The following day, on my sister's wedding anniversary,
a fifteen second window of opportunity aligned our
meeting. If I had not have slipped into my flat shoes
after work, I wouldn't have caught you. If you hadn't
have taken the different route home, I wouldn't have
seen you; but I believe in magic and so do you.

Paths

I walked into you out of the blue.
A sunny day where positivity and good vibes obey.
We believe in magic and trust in divinity;
On the same path, we might say.
We can share open hearts and words with meaning,
A new loving friend of earthly ways.
Sometimes it takes two to do what you need to do.
Let's meet, talk, learn each other's dreams,
Over lunch or a walk with bluebells and streams.

*I was walking behind you, excited I had spotted you
after such a long time;
not close enough to speak, I thought to myself, if you
were to turn around
then I would say, 'Hello'. You looked round, I waved
but you didn't recognise me.
I reached my parked car and as I drove by, you
signalled to say hello and I wound the window down.
Our meeting was like an internal firework, an
explosion of energy.
We sparked, exchanged cards and this is how the
universe brought you to me. That inner guidance, that
nudge that told me to take a card, was a split-second
decision that changed reality.*

*Have my ethereal feelings become true?
It's as if my dream man fell from the sky and he is
you.*

Future

How can you look into my eyes and see the water?
As strangers, I knew you were my future.
Creative in our own worlds,
All we need to connect is to put pen to paper.
My Aquarius air is a restlessness;
Your Capricorn earth is stillness.

I've had a disillusioned view from the past when it
comes to romantic relationships;
bringing yourself is enough. I've realised you don't
need money, you can create time, just keep yourself
open and listen to your intuition. Live life with love in
your heart every day and see how different your world
becomes.

Lucky for some

Thirteen days blown away,
With a bond so strong
In this world we don't belong,
Because we are the universe.

*Does it matter how long you've known someone for, to
question how you feel?*
*I believe in instant connection, that feeling, an
instinct.*
*The next time we met you walked me to work, I was
immediately comfortable with you.*
*If you had said, there and then let's jump on a plane
and go somewhere I would have said, 'Yes'! I held
your hand as we crossed the road, we kissed. There
was nothing else I needed to know.*

<u>Falling</u>

I'm falling for you,
As if Autumn has come early.
Multicoloured leaves floating from the trees,
A spark of Jamaica brings yellows and greens
To fuse with the earth
In a deep, red, sensual, layered bed;
Creating magic and passion.

We're so fresh and new, I want to learn all about you.
There is so much I already feel; only in dreams can
this be real.
Have I captured your wild heart?
Man of the earth, mind of the universe.

<u>Raw</u>

I'm wearing your scent like animal skin;
Musky oil and masculine.
I'll parade for you in Zebra print;
Tight, to feel your feminine.

Freedom is everything; an open mind is an open road.
An open heart is an open door. You let me in and I
want more.

Tender Hearts

We're tender love with dewy eyes,
Our passion lights the darkest skies.
Warmth and beauty hand in hand,
Behold the future in far out land.

*You're the one who keeps my feet on the ground and
head in the skies.*
*Is that not the perfect disguise? When I dream, 'I want
it now', let your patience infuse me to live in the here
and now.*

Heart shaped

I invited you to share my space.
Warm, open and full of beauty
We're heart-shaped lovers
In a quiet cocoon,
Sleeping, dreaming,
With a full moon rising.

*I invited you to my home for the first time; an
Edwardian stone building sat behind wrought-iron
railings.
A view of tiles and chimney pots frames trees that line
across the grey sky.
Below is where the bus stops in this regal named
street;
a place you've happened to pass many times before,
seeing my face, on the way to this market town.*

<u>Unmade</u>

We make a love that binds without chains.
I'm still learning to feel free,
You encourage to 'just be'.
Natural is the only way
To accept ourselves and have freedom to play.

My beautiful man, you move me like an emotional hurricane.

Black & White

I deserve to be me,
I deserve to be free,
I deserve to be black,
I deserve to be white,
I deserve to be a woman,
I deserve to be a man.
We deserve to be equal without a fight.

We're from different continents.
The Atlantic is the water that joins our hands;
Different cultures, embracing universal energy.

Before we met, I had a trip planned to mainland
Spain;
Sat at home with my map of Andalucía.
Six weeks later, we were on the plane together
to explore a new future; cooking up magic,
 writing on the rooftop, inspired by nature.
This was our first time away, but not a holiday.
It was to envisage a new way of life;
will this be the future I've been dreaming of?

A New Province

I view a white-washed village in the distance
Amidst the Sierra de Gador.
Moroccan colours line rooftops,
the warmth of terracotta beneath my feet.
A pink halo forms in the sky.
Mountains become a live canvas
fading pink to blues then grey.

And in a timely manner whilst at the stay in our cave,
I hear the publishing date for my first book has been
set.
Taking a long deep breath, this is where the interior
becomes exterior.
This is the coming out into the world and becoming so
very real.

<u>Walk</u>

Sexy and stylish, side by side.
Every colour skipping by.
We are the universe, infinite energy.
You've mastered 'in the moment'.
I'm your apprentice, mine is by the hour!

Let us be reminded to live in the moment and embrace all that is present

Footprints & Arrows

You leave a footprint with souls you meet.
A word speaks truth as an arrow
straight to the heart.
That message, an epiphany,
the seedling starts to grow;
an embryo. When it's ready to present, it will show
your words are your essence.
We feel them with power,
I'm in awe of your beauty,
The breeder of creativity.

*You're the spark that moves, with every footstep felt
with every heartbeat.*

Not just numbers

First day we meet on the street,
Fourth week our family meet.
Six weeks at 37 thousand feet,
Fifteen weeks my heart beats.
With you inside I come alive.
Who's counting numbers
In this infinite universe?

*If you could see two souls, how would we see each
other? Exactly the same.
We can only feel each other as deep as we've explored
ourselves.
Opening up to our truest authenticity,
Forever learning and growing.*

<u>Corners</u>

I pass the spot where we say goodbye at night,
Wrapped up in an afterglow,
Kissing like teenagers again
without self-consciousness and anxiety.
Liberated by our sobriety,
Age improved,
no airs and graces.

Your silhouette leaves me as beauty, etched in my mind.

Wild flowers

I'm observing the landscape as if I don't live here any
more.
It's been a year; with this is mind I'm already gone.
Blown away in warm air,
Scattered like a wildflower in the wind.
I want to sit in the stillness you live in;
Rest my mind and breathe you in.

A move is in mind to sunny climes,
a place for my soul to rest;
with sunshine and an open view.

Near but Far

I'm as high as the birds with you,
Destined to fly away to a town
where we've been to rest and play.
And as long as the sky is blue
I'll be thinking of you, mountain springs
And the land with the far-out view.

*You can fly a million miles in your mind and not walk
a footstep.*
I can't get the seed out of my mind, that I've planted.

Strings & Flesh

Wood, strings and flesh;
Sounds to dissipate stress.
Do we know our value?
Do we know our beauty?
When we're busy inside our head
How are we seen on the outside?
When you're a melody maker,
The heart moves the mind.

Our time behind closed doors are two open minds with open hearts; real time. You strum and go with the flow, I sit on your bed and think of words that syncopate.

Loving Light

Wrapped up in electric skies,
lullabies behind the eyes.
A spark of brilliance
lighting black and white skin,
Cocooned in warmth, embraced by beauty.
Beholder of the stars, hands that earth the ground,
Two lovers of the universe, with a unique sound.

It's bonfire night, the lights are bright outside,
all we need is the light held in each other's eyes.

Starry eyed

Everyone was there;
Opening night, shining bright.
A day spent like a celebrity.
No hiding behind the microphone,
My new world dream began.
Be brave, as my heart beats out of my skin.
Now I'm in the window and on the shelves,
Arrived as the hometown news.

Be brave and remember you are the keeper of your thoughts.
Do they hold you captive or set you free?
Release them and become a facilitator of your dreams.

Focus on one thing you aim to achieve, set the plan, and the universe will find a way to make it happen. Release the doubt, release the fear; this proud day in November marks the launch of my first published book.

A creation that connects through open hearts, to be passed through the family line and forever documented in time. Being birthed into the world of words is truly a blessing.

Soar

This is a space in time.
Like a bird you've given me wings;
freedom to fly, freedom to move.
We have ease and both fly free
Independently, together;
And what will be will be.

*I've felt pressured by my thoughts in wanting
something sooner than I can have it, in the meantime,
reminding myself freedom is a state of mind.*
*Feeling freedom is having choices or making moves to
create them. I've felt restricted in the past through my
actions that have taken choices away and through the
economic recession, when things are good, you think
they will last forever.*
*Now, the fear has returned in that Brexit could do the
same, as if my dream will be sabotaged in some way.
I'm almost ready, please don't take future choices
away!*
*Let us unite not segregate, let us have freedom of
movement.*

Moving On

Its nearly over, light at the end of the tunnel.
Good to remember where I came from;
blind escapism to a place of optimism.
The darkness can shoot up your spine.
Lessons learned are highs and lows.
We can't have it all, all of the time.
Times are changing, keep on moving.

Instant gratification in the form of over-spending
swallowed up my thirties and took away financial
choices. Born out of emotional escapism and having
learned from self-imposed restrictions, you can't sit in
melancholy. Whether we carry a burden of our own or
live it through another's eyes, the shadow of darkness
can appear, a reminder of where you came from. Now,
I dream of self-sufficiency; nobody supporting me, live
with what I earn and manifest what I need. You get
where you want with hard work, not when consumed
by greed.

Some days I would carry it heavy in my heart and
other days, fluffy like cotton wool.
Only through loss can the gain feel more precious,
And through awareness and change, bring the wealth
that is not money but knowledge.

<u>Your World</u>

When lost in your beautiful world,
You have papers for company;
Pages of wisdom occupy a place in time.
You're inside my mind, my lover of another kind.
Amongst a sea of books;
Poetic sailing with wood and strings.
Moody in your style, breathing beauty in.

Thoughts of you, my lover of freedom and equality for women.

Light up the sky together

It depends on the light
To accentuate your brown-blue eyes.
Meeting you dark skin was an awakening.
How the universe invited you and I
To travel the skies together.

Experiencing new landscapes sets my mind free.
I dream of living on a narrowboat taking in the ever-
changing scenery;
And a foreign getaway where you can walk barefoot
and feel warmth on your soles.

Sweetness

I want to climb in bed with you;
Touch you, smell you,
Wrap myself around you.
It's been a few days.
I'm missing your warmth,
Cheeky mouth and eyes.
Milky coffee is your sweet surprise.

*You are my sweetness; once I have a taste I don't want
to leave!*

Lovers

Curves that need no eyes,
Hand between the thighs.
A lover's glance at entry,
Then take my breath away.

We create lines that chase the day away.
Moments of sexual longing,
When you wish you could stay.

Sensual seconds linger.
That desire to be closer,
The dart of pleasure,
Let us dance and play forever.

Lovers engaging in a sensual art of play.
Bodies expressing love in an intimate way.

<u>Travel</u>

I'm reading into the photograph,
Seeing what I want to see.
All pretty is my perfect reality.
My own fields filled with almond trees;
Or, is it just today's fantasy?
Craving rural scenery seems to be a part of me,
Not just be on the map I see.

I want to fly away like a butterfly with wings;
restlessness speaks.
When was the last time I felt free?
I'm looking through Spanish properties.

Like Monday

Been pushing too hard.
Suffocation feels like
Deadlines and responsibility.
Seasonal germs are spreading,
Cold and dead on your feet.
Let me make it through the week!
I just want to go back to sleep.

I don't want to feel like a fish, caught in a net,
Living in a media fed society.
I hope to swim away, despite Brexit anyway.
It's like treading water, the day to day,
uncertainty can feel like entrapment,
when frustration and negative self-talk arrive.
Tears form a way to release and clear the air.
For a minute I was trapped by circumstance
Out of my control,
So why try and hold onto the reins?
Trust and let it be and add 'note to self',
To not to take life too seriously.

Rain

It's at the window, soothing and therapeutic.
The deeper noise is not my mind,
But traffic on the periphery,
Bypassing around me.
Whilst I am dry,
Rain is showering the earth to keep us alive.

Sow seeds

Sow seeds wherever I go,
my soul runs free, I have no home.
Staying in one place I lose control.
Find me a new place to take my soul.
I'm a restless spirit, gypsy in nature.
Writing is my mind's outlet where I become whole.

*It's time to sell my home in the UK for a casa
Española.*
My flat has become more of a bed to lay.
*Paintbrushes have dried, restoring elegance and
beauty,*
ready for someone to make their own.
*The past year's focus was to work hard, spend little
and restore the place I was calling home; because it
didn't feel like home anymore.*
*It was slowly breaking; roof leaking, no central
heating, a plug-in electric heater was my saviour, with
ski socks and jumpers to get through a bleak winter.*
*Hot water was a kettle for washing up and I still had a
shower!*
*I sacrificed and gave up expensive hobbies, seeking
cheaper alternatives, coloured my own hair, choosing
tea and coffee to experience the ambience of high
society without paying for a three-course meal and a
brandy, I drank less, stayed at home and ate more!*
*Slowly but surely it becomes homely and ready to
market. A part of me still wanted to see if I could
afford to stay; financial advice gave me the push to
finally say, don't keep paying a mortgage when I'm*

hardly home and have pressure to pay. Why stay comfortable? I'm taking another trip to Spain.

A New Home

Observe and experience.
Feel at home in a foreign land.
We are united,
Not divided by language.
The message will translate
When open to communicate.
Love is universal;
Sense, joy and wonder.
Feel the warmth in a smile,
In new faces we meet,
The colour of our skin,
Language we speak.
Where we reside
Should not define us.
Take away the thought of barriers;
We can be limitless.

Experiencing life as a lone traveller.
But I am not alone. I'm under the sun, moon and the
stars.

Solar

My soul has been recharged,
Solar powered by the sun.
I'm on a high as if the new adventure has already begun.
Feeling independent and empowered,
Even the British weather can't bring me down.

Experiencing what the future might be like has been
liberating.
I've come back feeling free. It's now late summer;
Still a few weeks to feel the UK's falling sun.

Lake Story

Experience peace
infuse with your surroundings.
No chitter chatter of mind,
Only the birds,
Wildlife undercover.
You could soar the skies as a bird of prey,
frolic with the moorhens on the lake.
Watch a dragonfly as it sees in multicolour.
Change perception even for an hour.
The lake will show you a new view.

*I can sit at the lake and dream away, to live in a
chateau, a boat or a cave.
A new life breeds, day, night and in my dreams.*

<u>Corinium</u>

How many times have I walked this path?
This familiar ancient parkland,
Lined with giant horse chestnuts and pines.
Warm breeze through the trees,
Let vitamin D soak through my skin.
Take a walk and breathe peace within.
When summer's gone, I'll find a new utopia.

I live by the moon with a head full of stars.
Walking the earth brings me back to ground.

Observe

Appreciate finer detail,
aesthetically pleasing to the eye.
Written word that breathes
an air of beauty across the mind.
Spoken word in a foreign tone,
breeding romance and sophistication.
Warmth beside a smoky lit fire;
Watching strangers lost in each other's eyes.

An hour in the life, observing society.

I feel best on the move; alive, freedom, exploration.
Yes, I want roots, but does that mean staying in one place?
Can it not be found when on the move?
A home will become my home whether it is native or foreign land.
My inner gypsy doesn't want to fit into traditional society,
And this will be my way of living a life by my means, without a mortgage.
Working with more freedom, no fixed home in my birth land,
but for the very first time I'll have a place I can truly make my own.

How often are we consumed by wanting something we don't have?

We all have something that someone else is looking for.
It's easy to look and think the person next to us has it all,
But maybe we have something they don't have, despite wanting something else.
We are blessed to be alive and for the moments when we feel alive
our bodies are temporary; it's our soul that's forever.
I'm seeking the path that feeds my soul,
that makes my soul sing; a new reality that I don't want to escape from.

House Sitting

Temporary companions, new responsibility.
Sights and sounds, relax with a purr,
Powerful felines, they know how to control.
I'm an obliging servant to make them feel more at
home.
Whilst Mummy is away, I'm their surrogate today,
Finding a way to connect and play.
A rest in nature at peace with the trees,
New scenery is a breeze to blow any cobwebs away.

I've started to house sit locally;
a sense of reward and warmth to be in
company of kindred, spiritual, feline family.

Mother Moon

Isn't nature beautiful?
You can count on the full moon
not to dim its light until the sun rises.
You can see imperfections in its light,
And be in awe of her beauty.
You can gaze from any viewpoint.
We all have a unique view.

*I see your light through the undressed window, across
a car park in this Cotswold town.
Whilst someone is wishing they could roam the sky
with you.
Others gaze at the comforting safety of your powerful
glow,
Hypnotic, teasing yet reassuring from their bedroom
window in the still of the night.
Take a look, where can you see the moon from?*

Almeria

Take me on your open roads
I'll drive the A-92N across Almeria
Where the air is warm and dry
And less light pollutes the sky
The roundabout with the bow
Is the A-399 from Chirivel to Oria
A province with mountain landscape
With leopard like spots
Your large expanse is rugged terrain
Leads the way to my dream home in Spain

Message to My Lover

You've opened my mind,
Been my supporter and encourager.
The universe has brought us together.
Thank you for being my reminder.
By my side, always touching my soul
in heart and in mind.
My beautiful lover of an extraordinary kind,
Sending kisses on the wind forever.
Blessed are all the moments we've shared
and our future heartfelt when apart and together.

A sale is looming, a home in the sun is calling.
This is what I've created. I've not made it yet,
this is just my new beginning